MW00685024

# FACING OURSELVES IN SILENCE, Vol. 1: When Words Are Not Enough

By Robert J. Patrick

ROM Books
ROM Publishing, LLC
P.O. Box 2047
Houston, Texas 77252

ROM Digital Ink Press®
is a registered trademark of ROM Publishing, LLC

Published by arrangement with the author

Printing History

First Edition August 2015

Library of Congress Control Number: 2015946120

ISBN: 978-0-9861192-1-7

www.ROMPublishing.com

When we stop fighting ourselves and let our soul speak, we become free. Being free comes with responsibilities. A freed spirit must find and free another soul stuck in silence. Sometimes words are just not enough. We must put feelings into action. **– Robert J. Patrick**

In Loving Memory of Jannie Pearl, Keith, Ms. Georgia, and Turtle...thank you!

## Catalog of Poems

---

## Author's Note

Poetry is an expression of creativity. Writing is the vehicle for this expression. It all started with Phyllis Wheatley and Jupiter Hammon, almost 300 years ago. African-American literature has changed so much since those days. In the tradition of writers like Nikki Giovanni, Countee Cullen, James Weldon Johnson, Langston Hughes, and Maya Angelou, this book will explore a variety of topics.

We all face the struggle of life and strive to live each day as best we can. This is the voice of me, people I know, and people I don't know. This is the voice of a generation wanting to speak words into life. Sometimes, however, words are not enough.

## The Clouds and the Trees

I'm jealous of the clouds and the trees
They see God every day
I swear I pray I wish
But man, I don't get to see his face
They get to ask for rain, thunder, and cloudy days
Small things compared to my living everyday
Just once
I wish I could fly into the heavens
And twist God's ear
With the problems, situations I have to face
By then, the trees and clouds would learn
To cherish the opportunity they get
To talk to God everyday
So, that's why I'm jealous
And I hate the rain
Cuz if the clouds and trees
Didn't jam up God's schedule
I might not have to deal with this much pain

## Under the Rainbow

Under the Rainbow
Where God left some of his children to grow
A place to abide in love and understanding
A place to pace life when it seems so demanding

In the fields, under the rainbow
I saw the whisper of a soul
That shined like summer in a midnight glow
Whose love for another, bold
I could not ignore

Whom, my brother implored
I did admire
Pure love, I could attest
Above their fire
They scattered and left
To pick flowers under the sky

Never could I understand
Nor judge my sister for her hand
I could only figure
That love has no limits
Judgments or religious overtones

Just a celebration of two spirits uniting
Just a meeting of the wind into feeling
So, let the rain come and wash the real sins away
Let the sun come out and play
And walk away from the clouds
To smile under the rainbow

## The Genesis of a Love Forgotten

With open arms
My hands wait for your warm embrace
My eyes start to water
With the tears of your love
Your arms touch my shoulder
And I feel the touch of GOD
With the heavenly rains
That cleanses my soul
Of the dirt from past loves
Broken hearts and lonely nights

Death could have taken my life many times
With the filled glass on the table
With the pills from the bottle
Or the gun in the closet
The demons of the past circled my head
I had no way to go
But in my soul
I was safe

When you came into my life
And gave me love
You unlocked my heart
When I didn't know it was still there
I am now ready for love
And it is because of you

At times I hate myself so
But the light shined through my inner soul
And I saw what GOD has created
GOD loved me enough
To save me from my own hands

And delivered my heart into yours
So here I am
With hands to pray
A heart to love
And eyes to see

My mouth pauses
To say, "I love you"
Barely breathing
My heart takes a bow
To your eyes
And absorbs the magic in your soul
Love takes me away to a distant land
So we can become one being
Once more

## Waiting on You

Steady climbing
Hoping our love doesn't fall apart
Like the untangled webs of love never changing
Guess foreign trips and midnight meetings
At the temple of your familiar never failed
Love conquers all
But your sexy lips changed the rules
Life doesn't keep me interested anymore
Like ice cubes in the summertime
I got a million ways to express my feelings for you
So let me sacrifice my pride
And I weigh my heart in chocolate
So everyday your words can be sweet
As I live my life occupied
Waiting on your to come stronger
I want you to understand
How you make me feel
One time, I thought I was losing me into you
Two times, I wondered how the magic lasted so long
Three times, I know we can reach beyond the stars
So wave goodbye to the proud truth
And hug me again slowly
Stare at my eyes
And let the tears of afar
Never stay with the soul of a love forgotten
Nothing in this world can really
Explain on how I wait for you
To love me again

## Finding Forever in Your Love

Somewhere over the rainbow
Between your eyes
Our souls meet
I see the love
That has been missing
Funny how simply a breath of your words
Lift my heart among the clouds
Heavenly sent with melodic instruments
Play tunes, plunking my heartstrings softly
To the dance of the angels
Combining all the elements of God's measuring tools
Earth, the ground He gave us, to claim the land we have
been given
Water, to purify our souls to send blessings, upwards to
him
Wind, the cool refreshing summer breeze, to calm our
journey to the center of love
Fire, to symbolize the burning love and passions,
I feel for you
So now we have completion
The final product of our union
That is the way the world should be
But inside our love
The symbols of the Almighty revolve and rotate
In and out of ceasing

## She Is

She is on my mind
As I sleep at night
When my mouth yearns for her taste
My words go dry
I kiss her in my dreams like before
And my hands felt her chocolate body
Molding love in my fingers
I spread it over her spine
Her mouth made my toes curl
One by one
My eyes close
My lungs decompress
And I melted like ice cream
Sitting on the oven
I miss her essence and want her again
Those lips taste like Bing cherries
And her mouth was sweet as strawberries
When her juicy fruit touched my lips
The rush touched the back of my throat
And I got lost in her spirit
Some may can this forbidden passion
But I call this spirit cleansing
So at night I kiss the sky
Waiting on my love angel to return
So I could bless her love temple once again
Signed with an empty love note
I am ready to deposit all of me to her
Because she is more than a woman
She is ME

## In Name Only

Say it once
Say it twice
Echoes words that my mind cannot comprehend
Being stuck in this semi-circle
Neither designed
Nor created by eternal force
Had me drained
Empty like the honey jar in a den of bears
In name only
Do I realize Love never lived here
Just left some mail to fool me
As the noon bell rings
I can hear the birds chirping
And see the light dim upon the horizon
So as my voice broke through the silence
Like hurricane winds whistling in the night
Or flames of a broken heart lit for the last time
In name only
Could I call you love
And still not trust myself
To tell you the truth about it

## Just Smile

No Frowns around these parts
That's what the mouth said to the face
Yet the face did not listen
The lips dug deep into the jaw
As if to make its last stand
Then out of nowhere
The sun slowly rose to the horizon
All darkness seemed void and lost
Yet the gums were stubborn
And hiding teeth
The eyes looked down on the cheeks
And commanded the mouth to open up
Slowly, the mouth began to open
And the teeth pushed through
Surely, as the grass was green
And the birds fly in the morning
Did that frown leave?
A smile arrived to greet all
That passed by
So to chase away bad thoughts and mean frowns
Just smile
And the good times
Will come around

## Let Them Eat Cake

As the sun shall rise from its midnight slumber
And the dawn can hear echoes of the moon
How long will the cries of the oppressed go unheard?
When people walk quietly and carefully
In dubious arms of poverty and suffering
I say, "Let them eat cake!"

For me
Cake is not the sweet dessert baked
By your mom on that special time of the year
But the burning fats of greed torn asunder
Taste the bittersweet tears of humanity
As some ignore the true suffering of others
They need a reminder
That their suffering is at hand

So my brothers and sisters everywhere
From every corner of the world
From every barrio
From every ghetto and wooden shack
Shove cake down the throats
Of those greedy immortals

## Once Along Came May

I looked to the heavens and kissed December
And January poked her arms back at me
In February, my heart was shattered
But then in March, her love woke me up
My body sprung to life in April
With only the words of her lips
Then came May, the month of her birth
A great woman was brought into being
May, May, will you stay?
Or celebrate this lovely day
Or run from June too soon
To keep the Sun away
She laughed and I felt puzzled
Dancing on the roof of tomorrow
Waving at the glimpses of yesterday
She gave me a wink
And disappeared
Never to be seen again
Looking through the listless skies of DC
Exploring underneath the calm of the seven seas
Where is my May, today?
I say
But June came over and smiled at me
And I forgot all about her

## Loose Thoughts on a Midnight Train to Sleep

Didn't know my Life was an experiment
Got myself in another predicament
Feeling it
Like two loose cannons
But these thoughts that swirl
Will manage a collision for words to rhyme

I feel stranded
Like a lost pair of glasses
Cause I can't see through the night
Lost without a way to Damascus
That blinding, shining light
That's surrounding my Life
Feels like the world's crashing
And I'm out of strikes

But I got to change the rules to the test
Got to be the last man standing
Before my energy is used up
So, before I let the naysayers win outright
I'll rather take the red pill
So my mind can take flight

## A Conversation in the Solo Express

Having it out with no one
Is easy as ABC
Like being stuck in a small room
Without a large mirror to see
Changes your life forever
As your mind opens up to all the possibilities
You truly realize the power of imagination
Someone Anyone and Everyone
Meets inside you
And no one can tell you
What to do
Just sit back and listen
As the thoughts control your mind
Let your emotions lead the way

## The Bird Sung to Me Long Ago

My heart tried to speak
Before my eyes could behold
The peak of beauty
Inside my soul
When the rain fell
Upon my window panel
The sun rose
And the bird started to sing
The smell of everything
Started the tears to form from it all

I look upon the depth of night
And lived through my day as the morning waned
Afternoon settled right down
But no winter came
No snow
Just summer wind to lift my hopes
The voice of the mountains
Lifted my spirits afloat

Time to follow the mountains
Time to settle in my afternoon
Can't watch people's evenings and night disappear
In gloom
Spring eternal like fountains on the bay
And inspire others from slumber
To walk into the light of day

## EGYPT

Mystic Lady, set my spirit free into the heavens
Daughter of Memphis, wrapped me in the bosom of the
mighty Nile
Sister of the Pyramid, placed my heart in the sands of the
Sahara
I feel the oneness among my brothers and sisters buried
there
My soul has journeyed to the depths of paradise with the
sky
Brothers of the Sun, touch my eyes that I may see the
beauty of the rays, unharmed
Knights of Cairo, stand to defeat our Motherland against
the enemies from Ra
The Great Pharaoh of above places guardian angels in our
lives everyday
Listen to their words
Hear their calls
Walk by the faith of your father
Run with the strength of your mother
If you can't do either
Then crawl with the hands of usefulness
All of God's children
Gather together in his Holy Name
For we shall not be afraid anymore
We will link our passion, peace, and prosperity
To create a Love Supreme

**You are My Angel Now**

Somewhere beyond the clouds
You have been lifted to sky
But I don't understand why
This second?
This time?
But your minutes are gone
I hope you knew how much you meant to me
The jokes
The laughs
And all those little things

It is hard to grasp God's wisdom
And sometimes our faith is tested
Through hardships and loss
Or just trials beyond comprehension
Just a few of the daily struggles we all face
But I know after we ascend to the above
There is a place where we all can go
Where our heads are not bowed
And we walk the streets of gold

There is a place
Where love stretches from eye to ear
My heart is trying to heal
Knowing that tomorrow is coming soon enough
And that one day we will be reunited again
We got a lot of catching up to do
But until then
Don't worry about anything here on earth

I will carry the load
I won't cry too long
The task is at hand
And you are my angel now
I hope you know
I see you every night in my memories

Memories, that is beautiful as the sun
On a cloudy day
Like the rain replenishing the waters
On the entire Earth's surface
And your love for me
Is my purpose
To be strong and live without fear and doubt
You are my angel now
So make sure my prayers reach heaven
On a quicker route

## Here I Am

Bare and naked
When I talk to you
Mind, Body, and Soul
I am there to comfort you
To love you

I am not perfect by any form
I bleed, I cry, I worry
Sometimes I feel broken
With my flaws displayed on the perfect scale
Yet every morning
I get up
And try
Only to be a failure again
To pursue truth
And seek myself
From the guile of humanity and its frailty
Shaken but more stirred
I can remain solid in my faith
And steadfast in my love for family and friends
I am not where I want to be
But here I am
In your face honesty
And Guess what?
In God's eyes
That's enough

## Laughing the Day Away

Looking inside my eyes
I can see myself
Walking in the sun
Behind the gray clouds
Covered with the haze of the day
I saw a beetle with five orange spots
Touching the petals of a red rose
Leaning towards the ground
Brightly and reaching upward to the sky
My hands stretched
To smell the leaves
Falling from a tall tree
Sitting on the grass
I began to realize how silly I was
Lost in my thoughts and my mind
I feel asleep
Peace and blessings to the earth
Only dreams and lullabies await me

**Man in the Eyes of God**

Mere mortals lonely, meek and gray
Confused, destructive in his ways
Mere ignorance
Not recognizing the goodness besides him
Dark skies
Teary eyes
Silence
And not much talking
Lowered head
No movement or stirring
Lots of walking
Long lines of lies and deceit
Finally caught
No place to flee
Denial of fault
When mortal men meet the eyes of God
And his gates do appear
Gone without a trace
Empty
Left without a place to live

**The Blue Moon**

The blue moon is blue as the sea is wide
From the brown earth to the green sky above
Mama always said if everyone was the same
Life wouldn't be fun
The blue moon resides in a little valley over the red
sun
And the brown earth to the green sky above
Mama always said color made a difference
In the pictures we paint in life
But where the blue moon resides
The red sun comes out for fun
Where kids play daily and don't mind the green sky
Mama always said innocence is hard to find
But the children are the keepers of this valley
From the green sky to the brown earth
Where the blue moon rests above the red sun
Mama always said if everyone was the same
Life wouldn't be fun
So where eyes are closed
And minds are resting
We all go to the valley of the sun and visit our blue moon
Blue Moon, let us march home
Until next time
Or darkness greet us again

## Accidents Revisited (Let me find me)

I walk along the broken pieces of the puzzle
Living with the thought of fear
Robs a man of his true power
Accidents don't revisit home
They show up like old bills and dirty laundry
And you must deal with them
Before they take over your life

Accidents are like
A nation of millions stuck in the mud
Confused and bewildered
Ignoring fires lit among the wayward and wicked
Somewhere over a rainbow wasted
We will find our heart and spirit
While tears may cleanse our souls
Life will find wonders unbelievable
And discover grace and mercy unto
What beautiful a scene to behold
Away from those miserable nightmares untold

I seek abundance through prayers
Through meditation
Let me learn to look past my future winter
Hopefully, passion will spring up like flowers blooming
Yet I glazed at stars and forget
They are decoys
Distracting me from being young in the summertime
We all walk away from our dreams
Scared of failure and our very own destiny

Time traveling and waiting on forever to come
But we never catch the train
And if that wish ever comes true
We cry on the front seat
Endeared for God's everlasting kiss
Listening to the melodies of love
From the sound of angel's wings
We sleep
As the dreams of never
Are locked away in the deepest part of our being
We embrace hope with silence

## Life without an Audio Button

Before the masquerade ended
The night came so fast
And the day began so short
I have always been in Love with you
My heart was always a slave to your words
Our lives had only been a stage
For the world to see how you mistreated me
Yet, I played my role
Like an Academy Award Winner
The curtains slowly drape the floor
The Light dim as the evening ended
There was no last resort to save me
My emotions were so far away
Tucked away in the abyss of self-pity
Stuck, never to be retrieved
Can you believe that I would have given my Life
To see you breathe one second more
Silly of me to take your love
As a solid branch that I could walk on
But the evil in you
Would have let me fall on my face
Sometimes I wish I had never been born at all
But in the reason buried beneath my soul
The deepest...The darkest...
Brought my tears to the Light
And comets appeared in the SKY
I cried and finally...took my Last Breath
Happy Feelings raced through my body
And this world became NUMB

## Open Season on Promise

Another life lost on the street
It's cold outside
Like liquid nitrogen in twenty feet of black ice
Guns a blazing
Bullets are making halos
Innocence is lost
To blood clouds that wept
Eternal shadows behind it all
Confused in internal wars
Neither friend nor foe knows
Which way is safe
Or where peace can go
I cannot settle my mind to accept this anymore
These strange fruits have blossomed
Into bittersweet bedfellows
Love and Hate
Peace and Conflict
When will this upheaval stop?
Can brothers rest again?
Without fear of being shot

## Loud is the Darkness I Run From

To stand inside my mind
I had to yell aloud
But no one could hear me
Not even my soul could whine
I cried to the wind
But his words were crisp and cold
And the sun laughed at me
It burned my spirit whole

So I sat down
To experience the moment
Time became a beautiful companion
And I whisper into seconds
For the minutes and hours
Began traveling in space and time
With the mimes

**Land of 1000 Screams**

My words are hesitating to react
Like the jury in response to Mike Brown's death
In the land of 1000 screams
No one is listening to the voices
Just silencing the dreams

The mind is a drum
Where the beat of life speaks up
I remain afraid of what cries comes at night
Untouched from the heaven's lifted soar
The heart is banned in the land of a 1000 screams

In the hand of righteous truth
All is returned to the source
No more hurt, no more pain
No more sun days disturbed by the rain

In the land of 1000 screams
Troubles and struggles never last
Above a whisper
The perseverance of soul
Achieves much
Against the despair of depression
Down memory lane
Just trying to remember the address
And the journey all involved
Cannot wash away the blood stains

## What is this life of mines?

Why do I feel like a loser
Maybe it is in my human nature
To feel this way
Down back to the cellars
To feel some kind of way
See those getting rewarded for doing the devil's work
Tried doing the same fare
But my conscience couldn't break even
Where is there for me to go now?
I can see my humanity slipping away
But it is late at night
When my monsters used to attack my sleep
But now in my weakened condition
They show up at daybreak
Ready to destroy me
Ready to claim my soul
Do my guardian angels have a battle plan
for me?
Now when I am too tired to fight
Every time I look in the mirror
The past fades like dusk to a new dawn
No one sees me crying on the inside
Smiles are like invisible tears
Until the good Lord decides the next stage in my life
Hanging on a thread
Leaves your mind drained
Close to submission
Dreaming until my future comes true
Has robbed my present the right
Of living with any hope of surviving
Help me
Find strength for tomorrow
Yesterday is over
But today is too long to ponder its existence
Or can silence wipe my tears now instead

## A.N.G.E.L.   L.O.V.E.

Anytime
Negativity
Gravitates
Embrace
Love

A.N.G.E.L.


## L.O.V.E.

Love
Overcomes
Vanity and
Evil

L.O.V.E.

## F. E. A. R.  L.I.F.E. and  D.I.E.  S.L.O.W.

For
Everyone's
Afraid of
Reality

## L. I. F.E.

Love
Is
Forever
Essential

L.I.F.E.

## D.I.E.

Dodge
Ignorance
Everyday

D.I.E.

## S.L.O.W.

Savor
Laughter
Over
Worry

S.L.O.W.

## Sole Striving

Higher and Higher
Our souls are reaching for the above
The evil one seeks to defeat us
In everyone's spiritual sole strivings
Yet despite all of the attempts
It failed

Sole striving works like thunder and rain
But how do I turn the sound off
And begin healing my soul
This must happen before
My spirit reaches full ascension

Ice become water after the heat of life
Has dissolved its solid form
Humans are much the same
After the hands of the Creator has crafted us to our
expiration date
It is time for us
To fly like the birds and the butterflies
Once the flower has blossom and bloom
Its petals fall to the earth
And so Humans return to their origin of beginning

Sole Striving is the deepest desires for all that is right
Dark nights, when one is covered in mud and dirt
But searches for the light
Drowned in the water of pain and hurt
Struggling to fight back

And you muscle with all your might
All journey starts with a step
Before you are back on track
All hands reach for help
Must all stay focused, keeping their sight

## Calling All Spirits Home...

Join me as I march into the forgotten fields of promises
Scatter my ashes near the fire of latitude
And let them burn the eyes of my redeemer
No faults just prayers from a fallen son
To a prodigal Father
Seeing the mistakes and faults of a new tomorrow
My soul veered into the enriching Light
Blinded by the depths of my Soul
I sat back and ponder the divine comedy
That ensured my life
Cursed again
But not by the hands of my tormentors
But with the sin of my fingers
My mouth was maimed with the words of hate
Against the very blood that flowed through my veins
For now I sit under the tree of everlasting Life
Where the sky and silence meets as foes from a distant
land

## Encouragement for the Weary

What is love inside you?
For you to dream sadness
And hope for happiness everyday
Makes you feel like a stranger in a common land

Isn't this world a crazy place?
For tears to dry before they fall
It seems all but a stare
Where stars shine without the twinkle
In the sky

Or where the moon once stood
As the morning begins
The best is not the last
And the love within the universe
Is shown to christening everything
Under creation

When you believe in truth
No lie can prosper
Without the darkness first dying
It is a certain fact
That all light will travel to your aid

Never can you forget the minutes
Prayer will leave the folds of your heart upraised
I did not understand
My words could move mountains
But at last, my hope became strong

Your voice may shake like the weary
However there is right in your might
Against fear
We can prove our strength
In standing

Even with our hearts being full
It is hard to release the miracles
Bounded within us

We are told
We are worthless
Powerless and not needed
And the right help does not always come at the first relief
You are blinded by your pain
You are blinded by your test
But you are divine as the light is bright
Pray your power to sight

Just believe in the Love Supreme
And the Almighty will open his hands
For guidance
Take that last breath and fight on
For victory begins when you know
That the total sum of it all
Begins with you believing

## No Words on this Morning

Ashamed how the voiceless remain stubborn
Or how they crouch in fear
When the dreams of one is shattered
All are veered
How can holy people preach against
The same scripture that remains unclear?
Different revelations
Only a few years apart
Whose God is more God?
Where there is evil all over these parts
I don't care about your religion
Or teachings in principle
I just want to know who got a dollar
For a little kid's pencil
And who got the next job to help someone
Keep their house
Or who got the next invention
To advance human intelligence on space and time
No need to rhyme
And set shit straight
I don't care how righteous you think you are
The pearly gates aren't that great
Sad how you can treat your neighbor that you see everyday
worse
Than a deity or spirit that faith can only show you
In your mind
Let me draw this picture for you
While you put a caged bird in the closet to die
You find that same prison
Will be the one you rot from
And that death is much longer
Much more painful to bear

## Rhymes, Metaphors, and Beliefs Vol. 1

Feet first
Out the wrong way
Like breech birth
One friend celebrates life
Another one sleeps in the dirt
The beginning and end

It's funny how life
Declines then ascends
We spin
Like spiders with the web we weave
How big trouble comes
When we lie, cheat and deceive
Not people but really ourselves
Waste good years
Hanging our thoughts on the shelf
Dragging good people into our abyss
We love to give death
A forbidden kiss
Hungry for depth
And didn't cut the mustard
Following demons in our head
Thinking we all got covered

It's crazy baby
No shade in the summer
Burn like hell
No sticks to the drummer
No beat can carry us thru
Caught up in the rapture
Of the devil's brew

Kill our hopes
Kill our dreams
As we walk together in paradise
And forget our childish things

Touch unholy thoughts
But pray to the trinity in still
Push the cup back that runneth over
Until I had my fill
Speak mortal words in heaven's wings
Make these lines talk
And the music from my heart, sing

This is not a ratchet rap
This is a fancy talk
Beauty in the garden
Summertime, watching the corn…Stalk
Beauty untapped in further course
Love my family, my friends
And appreciate the haters more
Provide the endurance to finish in the end
Wrap my hands
So my minds won't wonder to sin

Any person who strives for good
Knows it's all in the highest
Some get stepped on
Thinking clothes make them the fliest
Not realizing it takes more to walk away from a fight
And understand
Despite it all
I just might
Find a helpful word today
Meditate
Let the breeze reverberate
How can some get left with nothing
And something be the sum of everything

How can some deities leave with questions unasked
While the leaders we trust
Never reveal their mask
Religious verses have their places
Through sand, water, and races
Everyone wants to be a king, a queen,
There are many jokers
But very few aces
Don't let me rain on your parade
Don't let me cancel your picnic
For while you are lounging
Trayvons are dying

While you sleep
MLK still has his dream
But no one snores to the beat of a captured butterfly
And no one sees the tears of a blind man
Character plays the simple symphony
We listen to
Heaven reveals all we know and believe
So, find where you are
Know where you are beginning
Dash until the end
For you are greatness in the peak
A miracle beyond belief
Something in a simple rap
Can make you smile and cry
So before you die
Give living a try

## Turning Sorrow into Understanding

Sorrow can eat at the soul
Until peace departs like a weary friend
Greet life as the gift it is
And pray for time to soften your heart to heal
But understand death is sweet rest for the spirit
We all run this race called life
We all must join the circle in the sky
And ride the angel led chariot to toll no more
Sweet rest is the love we receive for journeying life
Trouble drifts away as a stranger in the wind
Only peace, love, and memories of past bonds
Bonds that guide our spirit always
Until we become part of the heavenly host
So, don't worry about heaven gaining an angel
Just know their wings will flutter in your heart
Guiding you until your time will come
To join the same
So blessed as you leave these words
And apart into the songs of praise
Walk the streets of gold and sliver
Wonder and be amazed

## Inside Me, My Soul Yearns for Your Love

Dreaming of you at night
Brings me peace
And the courage to live each day
There is nowhere I would rather be
Than next to you dreaming of tomorrow
Holding you close to me
Until love melts my last bit of self doubt away
There were days when the sun would not shine
But I kept the faith
And reached for your hand
Don't leave me now
It is all coming back to me
Love, ambition, passion, and hope
But my spirit is fragile
So hold me close again
Until I am able to stand on love
Or on my own again
Please let me be bold enough to dream in color
My soul yearns for you
My spirit cries for your touch
Save me from despair
And stop me from over thinking about tomorrow

## Sum of the Spirit…Left to Dwell Near the Moon…Getting Along with the Ground

Down to the valley low
I had a talk with my spirit
But the devil overheard
Shades of red
Clouded my vision
Can't get along with self anymore
Until the daydreams go away
I can fight away the trouble
Once my fourth eye shades from the darkness
The winds will be changing
But there is no magic or cheap tricks nearby
To satisfy the memory of the monsters dwelling at the gate
I cried to a Phoenix to save me
Memories trapped in my soul
Urged my body to leave here tonight
With no chance to be stuck on tomorrow
I decided to become a Weary Traveler among the stars
Loosen my chains
I told the yellow dragon
Surrounding me with blue fire
Loosen my foot from the ground
So I may fly
Peace at last
Peace of mind to fight sorrow
For everyone I love
I fight for the demons that scare us everyday
Hallow between angels' songs
I embrace the heavenly grace
Promised to me for an eternal rest
At last, I feel tears
And become human again

## Trapped at the Bottom

Life is a bitch
Feeling like everything's rotating
From the rock bottom
Trapped in my own tears
Biting my fingers off
So I can't reach for help
Can't seem to fight the demons
Released from the semen
That brought me into this life
Screaming
Despite the fail
I work to excel
My name
Written in ancient scriptures
Decoded in phonics and pictures
Past the love of dead presidents
Life tough built veteran
No guilty conscience
Pondering whether to rob and steal
Instead of folded hands and kneel
Heartless from the cold clutches of fate
But still trying to walk a thin line between right and wrong
Very little black and white
And many grey clouds I manage to avoid
From a frown to a smile
I walk into the sunset
The hero I dreamed of becoming

## In Help of Freedom

Plant a seed for me
That tells me that all will be okay
Tell the red birds not to sing tonight
But let the memory of me
Be the daydreams of the ancient deities
Roaming the constellations above

Bliss begins with the soft laughs of a baby's day
Beyond any ignorance tempted by fate
It is old to dwell on water when the soul is dry
Always been a dragon hunter
Or an evil slayer
Even got some dragon in me
Nonetheless it is besides the rock
And outside the scope of reason
To realize the goal of victory
Is the thing I can't fathom

So plant a seed for me
Let the four winds carry me home
Across the plateau into the endless river
I don't care for dreams
I prefer the silence of sleep
And the drama of peace battling eternally
In my mind along the night time

Daydreams can go from clashing
To ruining reality without warning
The shades of green, red, black, and white

Can paint into visions no man can see
Without the height of the Almighty
Every eye blinked into slumber
Feels freedom from a memory planted
Long ago by someone lifted in love

## Beneath the Shade

Beneath the Shade
Is when my life was molded
Magnolia trees and the sticky Southern breeze
Echoed the buzz of life around me

Lost in a world of purple and gold
I became a fixture in the old buildings
And transcended traditions of yesteryears
I answered questions
Became a gourmet cook
And made friends for life

Had teachers who taught life
Inside and outside the classroom
I remember sitting on the steps of wisdom
And sometimes, not walking in the hall of knowledge
I dabbled in the arts of stupidity
Until I decided to grow up
And be a responsible man
I gathered my determination
And harnessed my will to succeed
Did four years of coursework in three
Brought my mama home a degree

Beneath the shade
Taught me life
Taught me failure
Taught me to enjoy the breeze
Underneath the trees

## Madeline and Pecans

The muse I live for
When I think all is lost
I look at her sleeping face
And work harder
Never did I imagine
The love we share
Would be so real
Your kisses knock me off my feet
I promise to always give you
Your favorite hugs

I am incomplete
Without your love
Into the oven
You bake so sweet
Makes me warm
To savor your treat

I hide like a child
From the pain of your eyes
My soul wonders how weary
Your spirit is
I debate whether
I can handle the cost
But know I can pay the price
Just believe in me
And I will be your knight

## Good-Bye

Why is this one word so hard to say?
Is it the laughter that we share?
That makes it so hard to breathe
Is it the hurt and pain
That makes our tears so hard to push away
Goodbye is a sad word
Something we all never want to hear
But we all shall have it uttered about us
Some hear it young
While the grass is green and full of life
Others hear it later
When the bark of trees has fallen off
And we use a cane to guide our steps
Before we say goodbye
Let's say I love you
Love you for the good times
And the bad
For all the times we laugh
And the times we were mad at each other
But in this time,
I will leave a message in a bottle for you
And say see you later
For the journey ahead,
Just got a little tougher
And I need you to save me
A seat for when we meet up again
Goodbye, my friend
For now

But see you later.

I always say...

## Million Hours in a Day

60 seconds in a minute
60 minutes in an hour
The whole world moves at the speed of sound
I am left to ponder the timeframe
For eternal blessings to rain out
Don't make me rock the boat
And drown in my own impatience
So, I will sit and wait for my million hours a day
To come sliding through

Clocks are clueless on how they run away
TVs broadcast the end of counting
Like its 1999 once again
No one can be confused on that tangent
If all the angles we seek
Are displayed in the hands of righteous thinking
Then time can be split a million ways

A million hours rang out
Like the forbidden comet touching the moon
Cast the gleam of light across the driven snow
One day should not hold this burden
But it must
So shall I inherit this debt
And take my place among the wicked
Assigned to count the endless sins
In hands of the judgment

## Missing Without a Care in the World

The life of pride went missing
And bloodstains were left in place
Many people were shocked
To see how pride met its end
Rumors said common sense went more peacefully
But it too died a violent death
He was strangled until all its essence dissolved
How sad so many people saw them die
Then said nothing to save them
Ignorance strikes again
So sad how our world is inept
In preserving the simple elegance of Life
Two red roses and a sunflower
To the Milky Way
Where mother's comet orbits
Out of sight and inside our mind
Forever
Amen

## Hookah and Tears

Hookah brings the spirit of the day
Inside my mind
But only to shield my tears from the sun
My eyes are full of disappointment
I thought life would be so much better now
Yet I see setbacks over and over
I see my mother's eyes
I see my granny's, brother's and sister's eyes too
Did I fail them?
Or did I put too much on my back
To represent my family name
I come from hard working, smart people
I come from street-wise, tough walkers
I put my friend in the ground years ago
And say if it killed me
I would succeed
Every breath has been put into that promise
Can I look at the sun?
And said I don't know why I can't shine
Why do clouds try to rain on my parade?
I know I have done some wrongs
But I have done so many rights
Where is the balance?
I seek serendipity
From the hands of judgment day
Of seeing my sun and my stars suffer so much
If I could sacrifice my moon and life
I would to be all I could be to them
My tears don't seem to paying enough

Dandelion wine is not bitter enough
To cover my sorrow
One day, I can look into a crowd
And tell young black boys like me
That you can persevere
Despite life and trials
Your day in the sun will come
But I can only imagine
If I had been born someone else
Those things in my present vision
Wouldn't operate in Murphy's Law
In singing voice, the hookah says it is okay
So, I listen
And finish this hookah with tears of unforeseen hopes
Yearning for my voyage to Atlantis
With that sweet child of mine
In the autumn breeze within my ear

## Stop Calling Me, A. Mistake

I was made in love
Over and over again
You loved it
But now, you ignore my cries
Daddy says I can't live in this world
And momma feels the same way

How did the feeling change?
I thought my time was now
I thought I had the promise to change the world
But I am here

Stop calling me, a mistake
I was made in love
You just didn't appreciate the gift
Anointed in the above
I see your fake tears
And hallow promise
But wait, until later
I will come back to be with you
And this time, I hope you love me
Like you should have the first time

*Robert J. Patrick*

## Let this be Said for Now

Kids now kill because they are bored
No one is safe in their lives
Liberty, Love and Freedom took a toll today
Didn't even tell anyone the price they wanted
Many stood in line, broke and confused
Together, we are now living the universal nightmare

Horrors don't happen on opposite shores
But right here in our very backyards
Children go missing and vanish
Adults lose homes built on failed hopes and dreams
We elevate to the sky
Looking for answers
But see no answer at all
We give our face to shed tears
Giving our full devotion to humanity
By living the full measure of life

All people walked across a bridge
Where the white gloves will not go
All will travel the unspoken road
Only a few will see out from the dark
I pray their memory is not lost
Among the tears and thoughts
Located in the rubbish pile of broken dreams

Uplift the spirit
For tomorrow is upon us all
Uplift our mouths

So our words can be an honor to life
And defeat the dream monsters
These monsters look to keep this nightmare secure
To haunt the good and living
We are not looking at shadows
When we step into the mirror inside the room
Will we fight back?

We can find the key
We can break the lock and chain
But we must release our fear and be willing
To search for it all
A hero who dies at the hands of cowards
Is still a hero we should honor to the highest
The coward should be the one we cry for
For they know not what they have done

**Woke in a Different World**

These pillows are not soft enough to sleep
And the summer does not feel like freedom to me
Largely, I stand against the sea
And speak to the rocks to listen
That sounds absurd like chickens on the bedpost
This world has become an oasis of stupidity and
foolishness

Where have the people gone?
Have the aliens abducted them?
Or have they skipped here in search of intelligent life
Trying to find inner peace
Is tragedy unmatched
The roar of the dragon disturbs the wind
And the softness of the temperature
Allows the sun to drain all of the mercy away

Maybe I can find an island to escape to
Or rid the world of this problem of people
However that would take too long
And maybe I will take the former
To live in peace finally

## Yesterday, I Cried Alone

I sat in the dark, wishing it all came to past
I saw the evils of fire engulfing the earth
Racism, Sexism, Bigotry, and Classism
All dancing around the head of the present
Happy for the destruction of mankind
Through its own hands

What logical reason would teach hate is okay?
What reason in the celestial galaxy would point out
 Someone is inferior because they are different
These fires must be extinguished before the house burns
The foundation on which America stands on

America, your house is burning
This fire is a five-alarm fire
But you ignore it
Like a leaf riding the current of the wind
Nothing will be left in the end

So, yesterday I cried alone
Deep inside my heart
For everyone twisted by the snares of life
Take the time and uncover your mind
Before it is too late
To save our house

*Robert J. Patrick*

## Until the Last Time

Until the last time
My last goodbye
Has been uttered
And the open window of Hope
Has been closed
I shall look upon the face
Of the one who enslaved my heart
My soul and my spirit
'Til the time
When I can be free
And love again
My eternity has passed away
Love does not live here anymore
It has found a home somewhere else
Fragments and pieces are all that remain

**Make Love to Me**

I love that girl
Her walk rises like the tides of the ocean
Type of girl that makes you change your mind on life
Met her at a club
Between her skirt and high heels
My heart was squeezed like a vice grip
I knew she was in a committed relationship
But one night
I didn't care
Felt kind of bad
But I went to sample her sweetness
And was overwhelmed by the nectar of her words
Her kisses felt like honey fresh from the beehive
I went to the bar
And got two drinks to help savor her presence
Now, I am addicted to her
It must be a dream
Or late night vision
But we are back at my apartment
And I have lust in my eyes
But instead, I tell her make love to me
She looks off into the moonlight
And I never wake up again

## Let Us Not Be Weary

Sun, Sun, immortal source of light
Hallow be that rays of mortal gladness
Please warm my soul
And touch my life
So I might do all to make this world better
For you to shine again
The people are sad
The people are mad
The people are set in their ignorance
Chained to a mental slavery unlike none before
Let our people break away
And free their mind
To evaluate

## Missing Our Three Brothers

They shot you
I cried when I read
I got so mad
I wanted to kill them
But their faces were hidden
All I saw was black and white shadows
My thoughts got lost in the grey
Trying to change the hands of history
I even beg to give my life in exchange
For all three of yours

Ignorance should be broken into a thousand pieces
And stupidity should be frozen to extinction
So, I read more to see other heroes fall
I swore I wouldn't end up like them
But I see myself going down the wrong way like them

I talked to God
And he told me to keep praying
I talked to Allah
And he told me to discipline myself
I talked to Buddha
And he told me to free my mind

The Wiccans advised talk to Mother Earth
But I do that everyday
Does that make me a heathen?
I heard the wind blow
But was afraid to listen

I thought my mind had finally cracked
In the search of peace and heaven
What the hell has become of me?

## S.T.A.N.D. or P.U.S.H.

Stupidity

Taunts

Anyone

No one

Definitely

## S.T.A.N.D.

We run into dangers

We run from sound advice

When will we P.U.S.H. back for reason and love

And for the Supreme because....

Perseverance

Undermines

Stupidity

Handily

## P.U.S.H.

## Caught in the Clinch

Simple kisses complicate
The thirst in my mind
For one more touch of you
Vast images replay in the back of my head
From the rain on the umbrella
On the night we first met
To your hands around my waist
Telling my body, it was loved
My fingers clinched and froze at the thought
Of being intertwined in love with your eyes
Your skin smelled of lit candles of strawberry and melons
Sweet nectar in the fancies of honeybees in the daytime
I can imagine my lips engulfing your lips
And the heavens smiling down on us
Just before the moon drifts into the shadows of the stars
My soul travels light years away
To speak cosmic to comets and constellations
Hanging in the back of thunder clouds and sun storms
Leading my whispers away
Between trees and deep passions yesterday
I listen to my body enter the arch of the your temple
And get lost in the mazes
That your hips presented my legs
When my heart started to walk
Before I could twinkle
My feet froze at the sight of the lava
Gushing from your soul
It was hot like the African Jungle on a midsummer's day
At last, I began to swim down and away from you

Into our everlasting forevers goodbye
Don't call this an orgasm of the conscience
But call it a unique collaboration of music strung together
In the eternal symphony
Never to be played again
My love
My sun
My everything
Face my eyes
And fall deep into my thoughts
Float like a butterfly
And don't drown in your insecurities and doubts
For the sake of us

**Music in My Feet**

Boogie with the rhyme of Life
My legs carry me thru the song
With the music in my feet
There is a fire burning inside me
To unleash on the dance floor
I want to be full of fun

And rid my body of awkward feelings
Let me groove with you baby
Let our feet take steps in soul patterns
While we are cleansed in the footsteps of our ancestors
Let their essence fulfill our purpose

We only come as kindred spirits of song
Christening life and struggle in this way
Earth dwellers may hear our noise
And wonder at the hands of the Creator
Let the Creator smile and delight
While his hands continue to play soulful rhythm in hearts

Spirituality is not a brand of music
But a bonding of souls deemed worthy
Of recognizing heavenly melodies
Absent of self and centered on fulfillment at the apex of
glory

So in the end, we control the chords and notes
And release our passion into our purpose
Only then can we be deemed cleansed in spirit

Until the music we make ends
We stand on the floor, moving our legs to the boogie of
rhyme

Robert J. Patrick

## A Penny for Your Thoughts

What is the cost for a sinner's redemption?
Staring at the mirror
I wonder the price on my soul
In the bible, it says it's hard for a rich man...
But reality, the poor get it much harder
Tumbling fast than a rock
Towards the stained glass in the church windows
I cussed so much
Realizing the bittersweet words I stored away
Were front and center
Speaking against the barrier
Silence had imprisoned me
Midnight is darkness
Like a night road over Arkansas
No starry night to guide me through the mission
Two hands down
Like I see the gun pointed
What to do?
At the lighting speed of brainstorming
Creation had a new reflection of the breath
Left in the heart of me
Holding on to my pennies
I started speaking loud thoughts
As the nickels hit the collection plate
The color of the blues
Were paid for by
The 400 years of oppression
My brothers and sisters continue to face
A penny for your thoughts

An earth blessing
Igniting the theory of Free
Pointing the gun of my fingers I made
Back at me

## You Have Been Warned

Your time will come
And when it comes
I hope you suffer
For the times a child starved and you did nothing to help
Tax write-offs and sports cars were your focus in life
Every house foreclosed
Is a nail in the coffin of your death?
Can't wait to spit on your grave
I hate you
And every part of your being
For the evil you have done to so many
Ripping out hearts and producing countless tears
Your time will come
So many people
Trying to do right and play by the rules
Get dumped on and laughed at by you
Even your pallbearers will leave you high and dry
So your funeral will be empty and barren
Like your dark and twisted soul
Today, we are gathered here
We come to celebrate the death of the American Dream
And hopefully put to sleep the nightmare lingering now

**You are My Everything**

Every breath of you
Breathes life into my vast empty body
I am in total mercy
Of your power and strength
And seem in awe of your marvelous beauty
You have rescued my soul from the abyss
Of tainted dreams and forbidden love pleasures
Rooted in continuous pain and mental anguish
Test my gentle loyalty
With a kiss from under the clouds
Sweet lips
Salute my mouth
With the privilege
No, the honor
Of being caressed by
Your essence, your inner multitude
From my flesh
To your flesh
Let eternal flames scorn and burn
Forever, trapped in an heavenly enchantment
Designed by God, himself
Keep us together
So, love can abide in the seams
Of our souls forever
If God willing
Let the heaven rain down on
Every limb and every morbid fiber
Of my being
So I can upkeep
This everlasting promise to you
My Love
My Funny Valentine

My Air
The thing that keeps me going
And the piece of me that lives on
Well after my being has gone away
And God has called my name

## Poem in A minor Key

Been whistling Dixie
And humming hymns all day
So the monsters don't get me
It was hard
Looking hard in the mirror
Walked blurred lines
But couldn't see any clearer

No priority needed
Standing on my own
But my ego is depleted
Not hearing the words
Hard drive broke down
But I'm hitting the curves
A foul intense superb
In rare form, now
Bump the nerves

Kissing a cat o' nine tails
Twisted and sinister
'Cause my tongue is so sharp
That this poem yells
Finish her
Denying the hail its spot
My hand is stuck on the universe
Yet the rain won't stop crying

Watching the sun run from the wind
Is like sound missing from a drum beat
So my soul fails to breathe again
I repeat
My worries are sweet
But my life
Is a strike on deck
However I can't be destroyed like a myth
Or energy
My soul just transfer
From genius to a greater entity
From comets to planets
My spirit has been stranded
So when you wish against all hope eternal
My thoughts can be seen from a telescope
Inside a kernel

**Depths of Truth Unexplored**

Lying has become a second nature in our daily lives
We look into dirty mirrors and convince ourselves
That we are truly happy inside and out
Even with our smiles tainted with deadly snares
We follow others
We ignore our inner voice
And fight everything that brings us the truth
Because in the end
The depth of ignorance remains delightful
Our soul remains unexplored
Our love remains hidden from other people
And the truth remains as the wind
In the Mississippi heat
While some of us find the shovels
To begin digging
Others never start the work
Too lazy to discover self

## "October"

It was a mid-October day
When you stole my heart away
The Sun beamed like a warm smile
Then the wind howled like a newborn child
The storms came and dumped the rain
My body hurt from your love
My head was dazed from the pain
Spirit drugged
Heart drained
Eyes closed
Feet froze
Confused, confessing my sins to the mirror on the wall
I purged myself from the evils of regret
But my thoughts stalled
The evil in my mind would not accept my tears
And my soul felt clean like a lamb
His eyes opened up like a million dams
Pray for me
That my light will not dim
So the tears of my father
Can cleanse my sins again

## Rage Against the Day

Losing faith in the light
And dying in the dark.
Where can I be free like the wind
And embrace the sun like an old friend?
Making the days count
Like a candle in the window
Surrounded in the cold and bitter truth.

Take me to sand
And speak the holy words over me
Wasting in the crack of the pyramids of time
Nobody can stop the movement of love
From capturing me
I am stuck in the beginning
Never to see the ending ever again

Heart so cold
It cannot bow to the Creator
Or any heavenly host sent to redeem me
That is the way of hate
When it feeds off the remainder of love
Love, left to die afraid and alone

## Just a Few Words in a Statement

Love springs eternal
Where hope remains afloat
Let humble eyes bow
Until lips meet as distant strangers
Good night to the soul of tomorrow
And good day to the heart that bids adieu

## On the Run with Nothing Trailing Me

I am a weirdo
Who creeps into the night
Wondering whether I belong here sometimes
A never-ending cycle of thinking I am not good enough
To grace the sun with this remarkable smile
But much like it
I have come to shine

Is it the deep down self-doubt
That causes me to panic
When I feel the smallest slight directed my way?
It is
How the introspect is flawed like the inclusions
In a diamond
But we fail to look past the beauty of misfortune
Searching for the fault within our broken fingertips

The souls of these words bleed
Searching for love and peace
Wanting to be somebody else's inner thoughts
Thinking about spending my life in seclusion
So my mind won't tempt me to change the world
I cry between hands everyday for my people
Stuck in despair and disappointment
They wave goodbye to their hopes and dreams
Hang themselves across the way
Hoping for a painless quick death
But everyday they don't die
And their hell is revisited

*Robert J. Patrick*

So sad how the sun teases the moon
And sky sits back and plays middle man
Just watching like no way out

## Calling the Kettle Black

Calling the kettle black
But another brother or sister dies in police custody
Quick to quote black on black stats
But slow to acknowledge the historical facts
Scream, my brothers
Yell, my sisters
Make your voice heard
A system designed without you
Was never there to protect you

Calling the kettle black
On the stove of injustice
Can only ignite the heat of anger
From years of built up pressure
I steam from seeing the useless deaths
I used the pen
I participated in the marches
I rallied my people to take action
So, this pot will not condemn anyone upset
But can there be a better way?
I just don't know
Sometimes, something must be destroyed
Before it can be built again
Sometimes, something must go through the fire
To be cleanse again
This pot will not call the kettle black

But I will say, "That justice must come!"
Medgar, Malcolm, and Martin all sought the truth
Behind the lies injustice has planted deep in the soil of
America
But they are not here to speak to the people
Whose fault is that?

## Determination

My strength is gone
And I have lost my balance
But I believe in me
I believe there is something good
Left inside my empty body
Everyday life beats me down
My legs ache
And my soul quivers
My arms shake like the coldest winter
The pain discourages me
Yet I will march on
Headstrong into my suffering
So I can fight tomorrow
Anew

**Wind**

A feeling, chilled over an emotionally charged gladness
Stirred with a bit of disappointment
And bitter sorrows
But set for success
Over a hot, humid day
The breeze that tickles my skin
In a unique way
I am in awe over it
This relevant but unseen force
Phenomenal, abstract cousin
Who plays host to gravity
Is the yearning freedom called wind

## America, I am Your Forgotten Son

America so beautiful
But ignorant in its ways
Searching the world for black gold
Wrong place today
But I know the other black gold
More valuable by the pound
You don't need any scientists to explain
Just look around
Some of the most precious resources
Lies in the mind of my people
We drew up D.C.
And made the roads safer
Benjamin Banneker
Garrett A. Morgan
Does that ring a bell
I see skyscrapers
No, I mean
Projects buildings
Reaching the ceiling
While the unemployment rate climbs
At the drop of a dime
Only hopelessness
Drop Out rates
Will rise
America, America
God shed his grace on thee
But not mercy
For the people you squash recklessly
We fight back
Vietnam
Korea

Latin America
And Iraqi Freedom
You think you are the liberator
You are just an occupier
While you travel abroad
And show the freedom
Of your light
I, A Black Boy travel blind
In the darkness of night

## Ebony Dreams

Cherry lips
Pecan thighs
Got ebony dreams
In my eyes
Buttermilk skin
Smooth like melted ice cream
She is my Campbell's Soup
On a cold winter day
The lawyer sistah
The church-going sistah
The teacher sistah
And even the poet sistah
Walking
Switching in perfect symmetry
Ebony dream
My ebony dreams are
For the midnight dwellers
And broad daylight
Brothers craving their
Ebony dreams sellers
And I smile on the way home

45597819R00058

Made in the USA
Charleston, SC
31 August 2015